MW01141112

WOBBLY WOMBATS!

OH MY STARFISH!

GREAT GUMNUTS!

ROOS TO THE RESCUE!

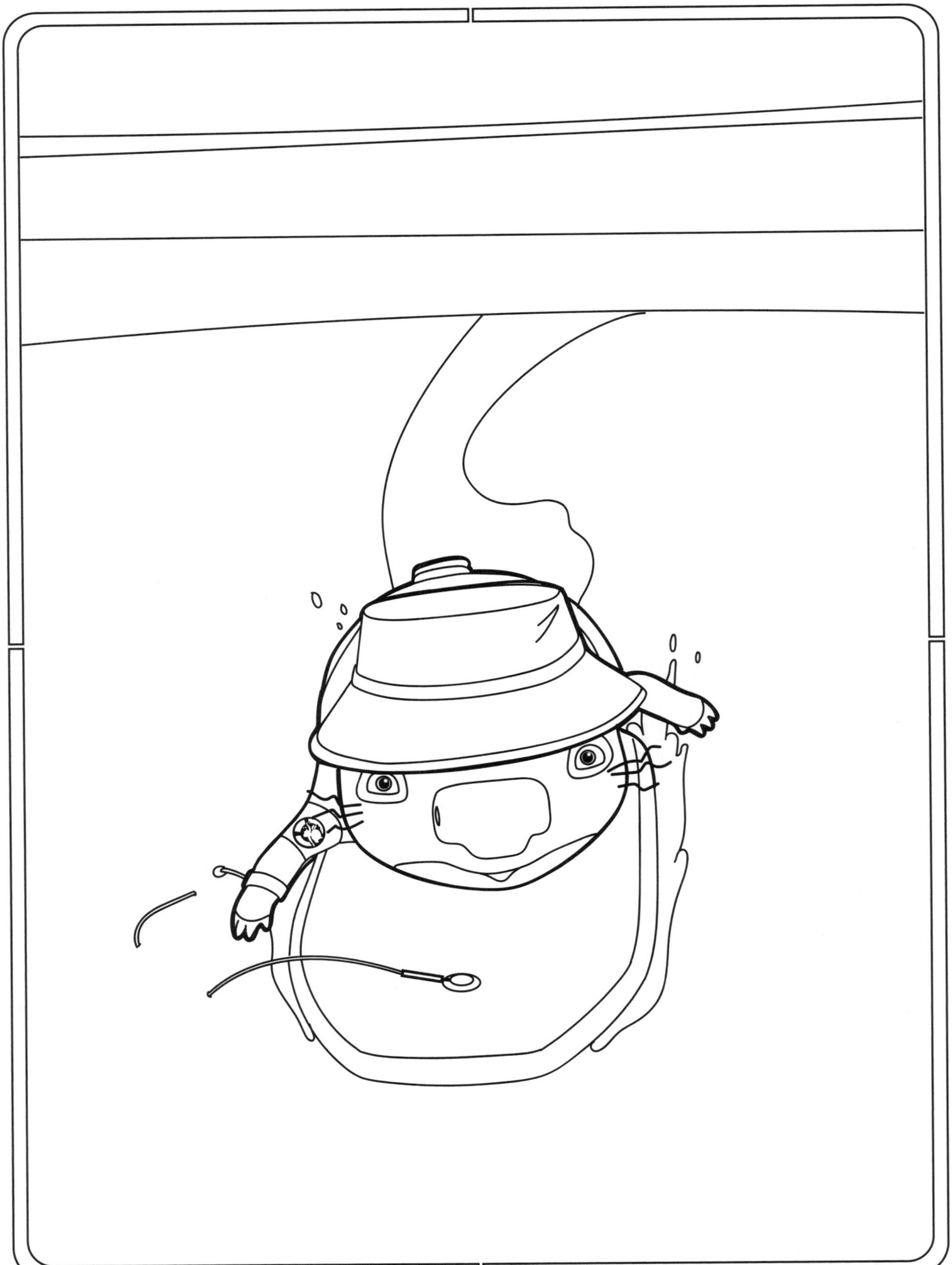

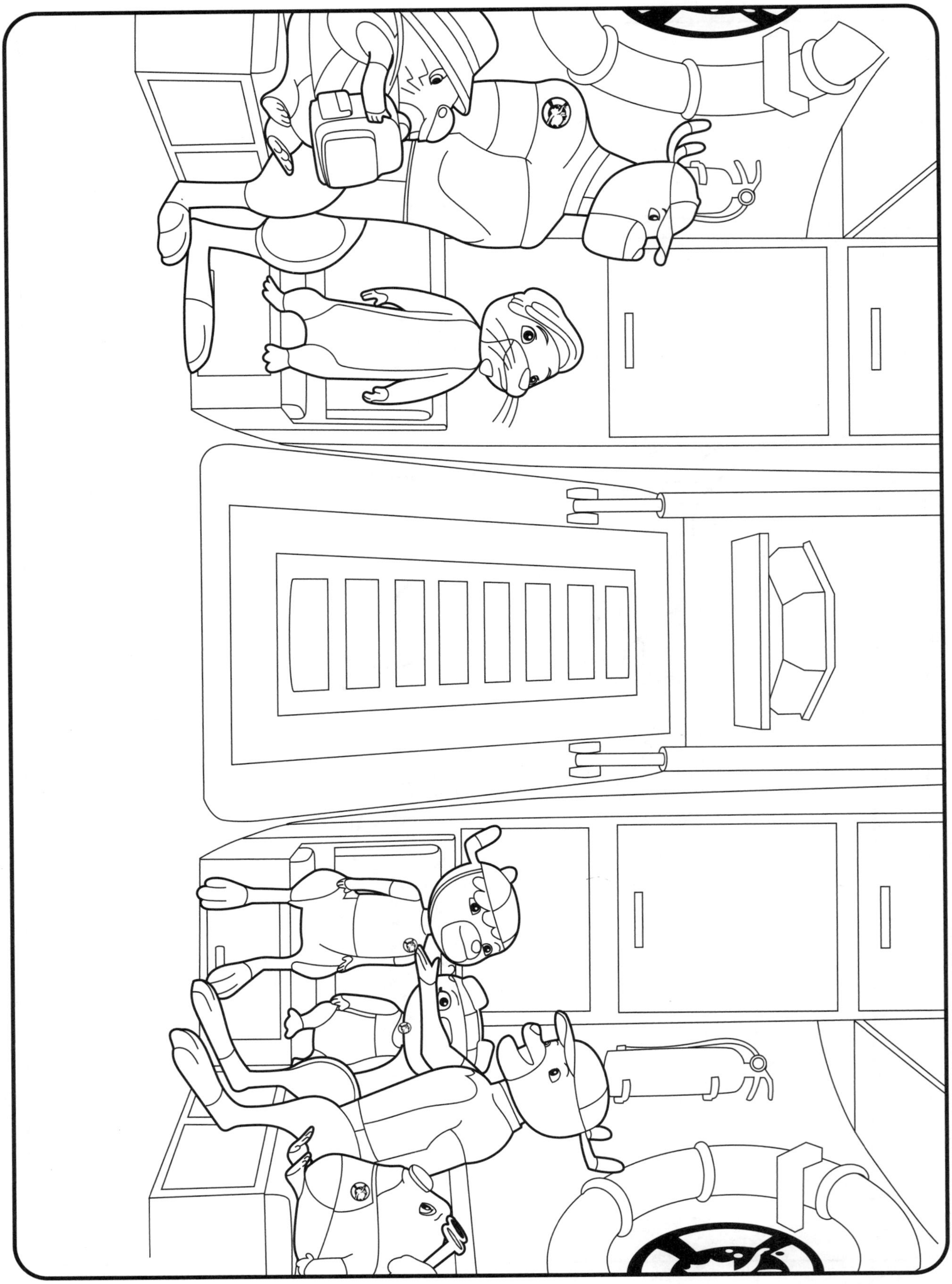

Kangaroo
BEACH

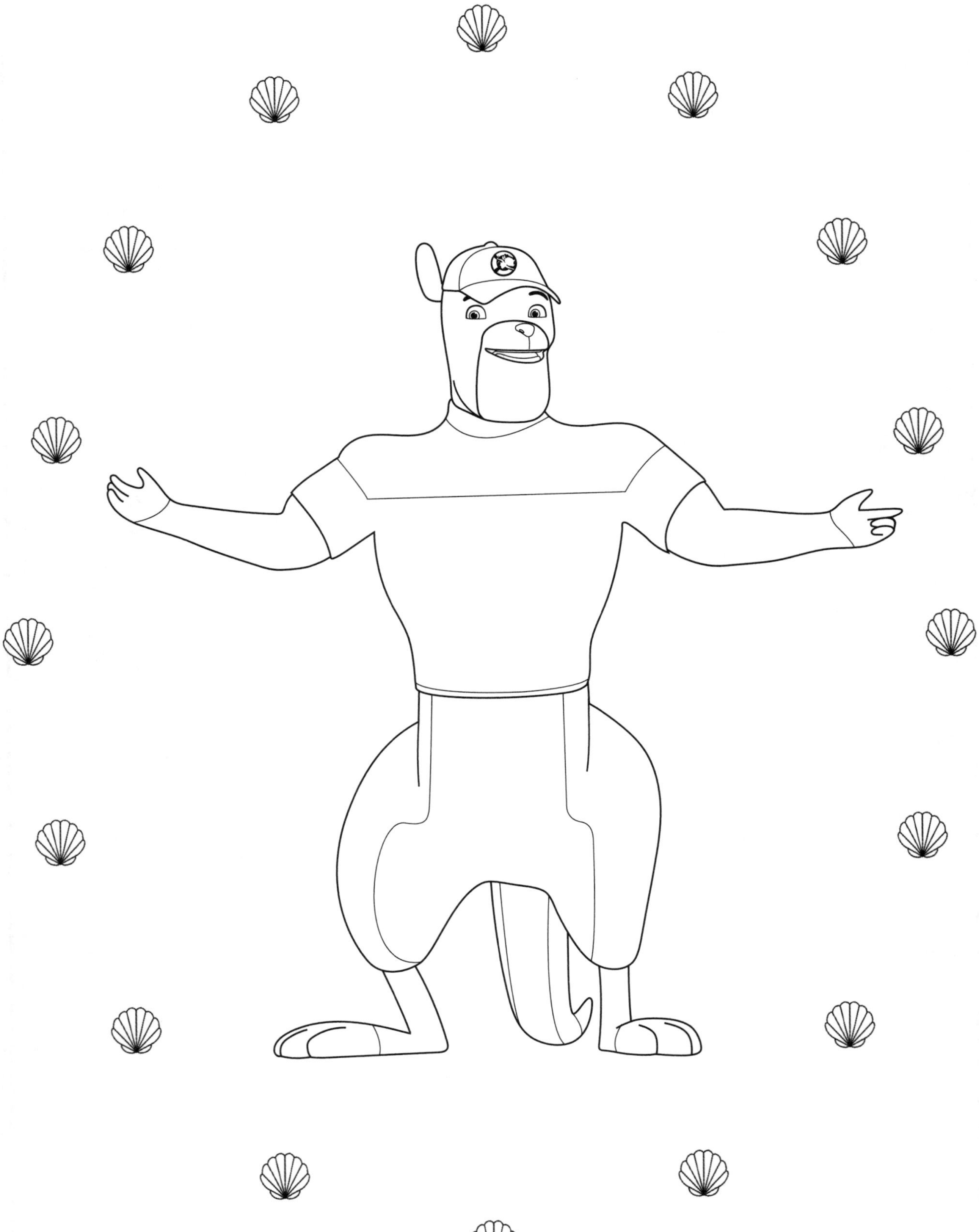

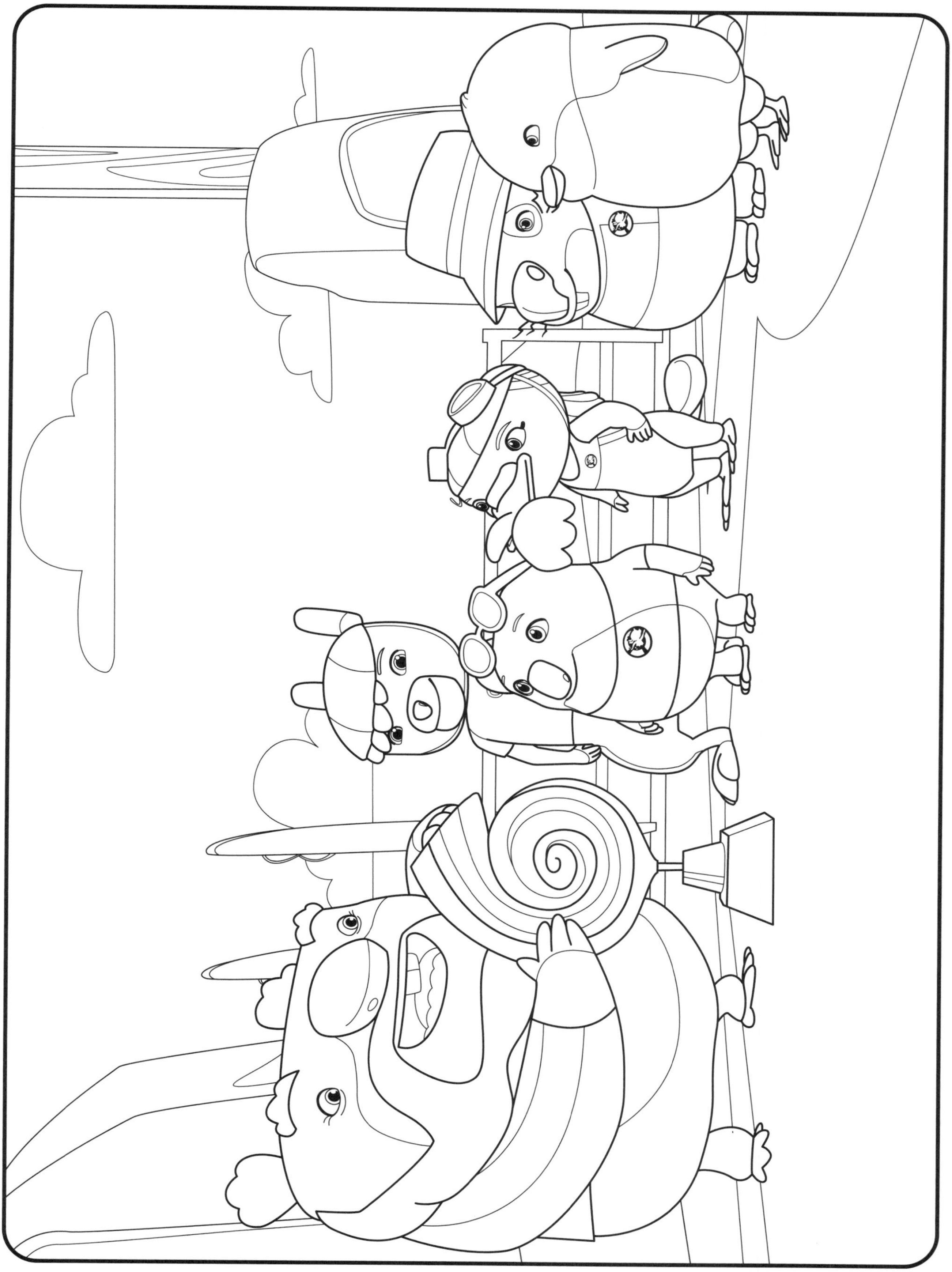

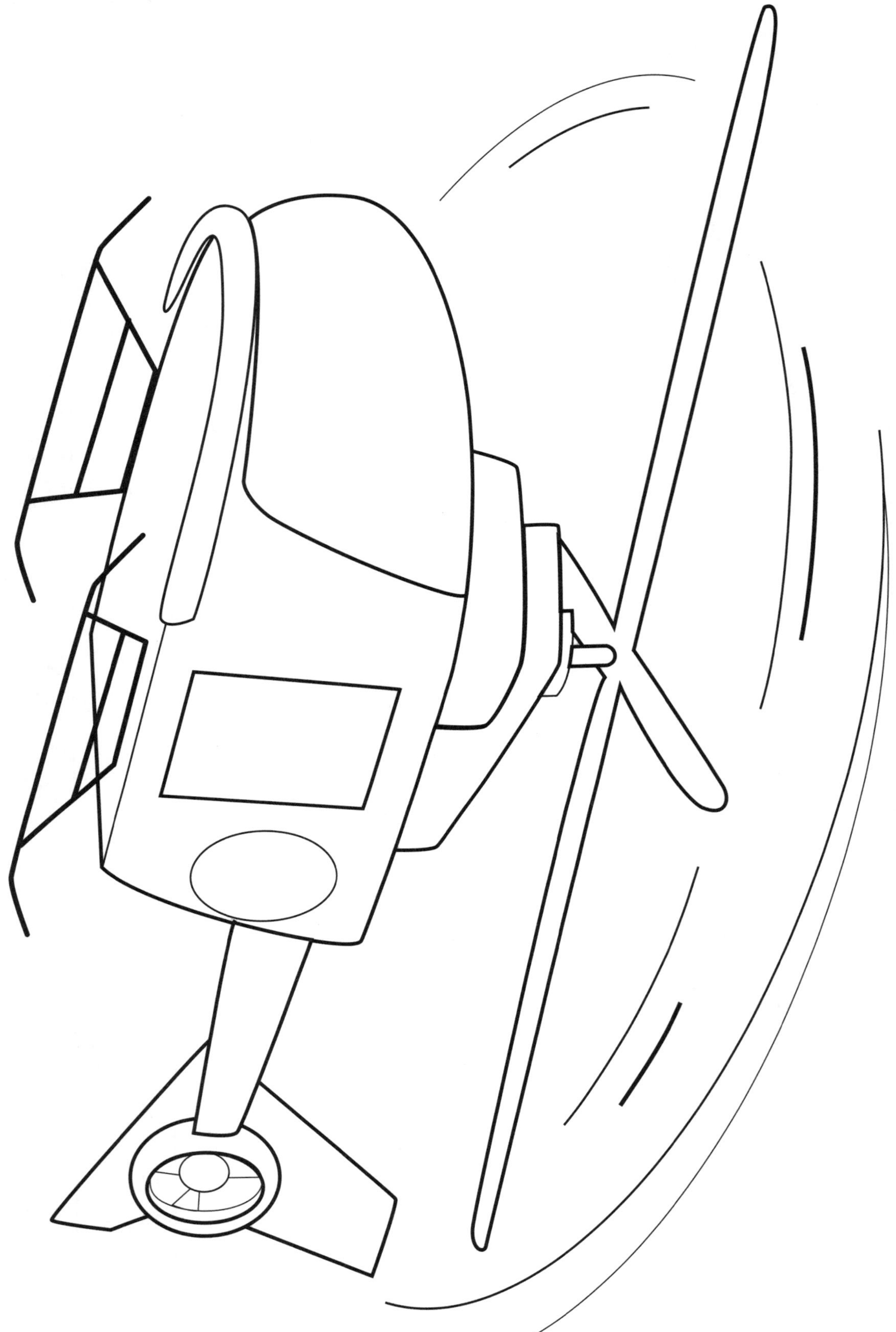